INCONTINENCE

A guide to the understanding
and management of a very
common complaint

DOROTHY MANDELSTAM MCSP Dip Soc Sc

Illustrations by Brenda Naylor

Published for the

DISABLED LIVING FOUNDATION

by

HEINEMANN HEALTH BOOKS
London

First published 1977
Reprinted 1978

© The Disabled Living Foundation 1977
346 Kensington High Street
London W.14.

'Heinemann Health Books' are published
by William Heinemann Medical Books Ltd,
23 Bedford Square, London WC1B 3HT.

ISBN 0 433 20260 2

Typeset by H Charlesworth & Co Ltd,
Huddersfield and printed and bound
by Redwood Burn, Trowbridge and Esher

INCONTINENCE

**A guide to the understanding
and management of a very
common complaint**

CONTENTS

v

CONTENTS — *continued*

ACKNOWLEDGEMENTS

I am grateful to Lady Hamilton, Chairman of the Disabled Living Foundation, who saw the need for a book of this kind and asked me to write it. My thanks are also due to Miss Sydney Foott, Editor of DLF Publications, to my assistant Mrs. Margaret Gillson for her untiring help and support, and to Mrs. Brenda Naylor for her sympathetic illustrations.

I am also greatly indebted to my colleagues in the Geriatric Unit at Edgware General Hospital, especially to Dr. Monnica Stewart for her encouragement and to Dr. Margaret Gray for her constant help and constructive comments.

FOREWORD

Leonora Elphick's pioneering book 'Incontinence: Some Problems, Suggestions and Conclusions', first published in 1968, is now out of print. It arose out of the concern of the Disabled Living Foundation with the clothing difficulties of disabled people of all ages, including the elderly, and aroused great interest. It was followed in 1973 by a second publication, a survey by Patricia Dobson SRN HV, which revealed the shortcomings and inadequacies of resources available to those coping with incontinence in the home. A third book appeared in 1975, by Peter Lowthian SRN, which listed portable urinals and related equipment, with a guide to their use. This fourth and latest publication, by Dorothy Mandelstam MCSP, Dip Soc Sc, Incontinence Adviser to the Disabled Living Foundation, will we hope bring greater understanding of the condition, and give practical guidance to more effective management.

The Trustees of the Disabled Living Foundation would like to thank the anonymous Trust which has understood the need for continuing and developing the Foundation's work on incontinence, and has provided the necessary funding. Our educational role is steadily expar ⅃ing, with nationwide conferences and courses for professionals on all aspects of the subject. We now offer a specific advisory service to those affected by incontinence and to those involved in their care, and, through the many enquiries which the Incontinence Adviser receives, the variety and complexity of the needs and dilemmas confronting both are constantly made plain. The knowledge gained in this way has helped to shape this book, and we hope that this valuable two-way exchange will continue.

The Trustees thank the Advisory Panels of both the Incontinence and Clothing Projects for their continuing interest, and John Brocklehurst, Professor of Geriatric Medicine at the University of

Manchester and a member of the Incontinence Advisory Panel, for his Introduction.

The Trustees are especially grateful to the author, Dorothy Mandelstam, who as well as being Incontinence Adviser to the Disabled Living Foundation also works practically in dealing with the problems of incontinent patients at Edgware General Hospital; she is thus highly knowledgeable on a subject so many find obscured by its unmentionability. The Trustees also thank Brenda Naylor, the sympathetic illustrator.

W. M. HAMILTON
October 1976

INTRODUCTION

Incontinence is a problem which far too many people have to put up with. There are many reasons for this, partly shame and an unwillingness to reveal that it is present, partly a feeling of hopelessness that nothing can be done, and sometimes because doctors and nurses seem particularly negative in their approach, and this often stems from a lack of knowledge on their part. So much has been discovered about incontinence during the last ten to twenty years that it is only now that medical schools and schools of nursing are beginning to teach their students about its implications. Yet incontinence is a symptom and just as with any other symptom (for instance pain, fever, vomiting or weakness) it needs to be approached with a full history and examination and quite often additional tests must be done to discover its cause. It is only once the cause has been discovered that treatment can be effective.

Dorothy Mandelstam's book is much to be welcomed because it constitutes an important attempt to dispel this ignorance. She sets out clearly and simply and yet in a comprehensive manner the basic causes of incontinence, how they affect different people, and how these different causes can be treated. She also presents information about a whole range of appliances, special clothing and so on which is helpful in the management of incontinence in those cases where it cannot be cured. She rightly stresses, however, that diagnosis and treatment must first be made, and if this is done effectively then the proportion of patients who will need to use appliances of various types on a long-term basis will be very small.

This small book is a mine of information and will be of the greatest use not only to incontinent people but also to those who look after them, and in particular doctors and nurses.

J. C. BROCKLEHURST
MD FRCP

1

Focus on incontinence

During many years' experience as a physiotherapist and social worker I have been involved with incontinence in gynaecological and geriatric care, both in hospitals and with people at home. Recently, as an adviser on this subject to the Disabled Living Foundation, I have become increasingly aware of the need for a greater understanding of incontinence, and for advice in dealing with it.

The purpose of this book is to try to fill this need. It is not a textbook, but its aim is to show that incontinence in all its varying aspects can be prevented, treated, alleviated, or managed with dignity, and that recognising the problem is the first step towards finding a solution.

What is incontinence? It is a loss of control over the bladder or bowels. How many suffer it and who are they? They are innumerable. There is the unhappy young man who wets his bed, the schoolgirl who has occasional accidents while giggling, the young mother who has had incomplete control since her baby was born and who, when she reaches middle age, will have even less control, and the isolated and housebound elderly. In addition to these, there are many people who are disabled either physically or mentally, and those suffering from an acute illness or injury. Incontinence is a symptom that may occur to any of us at any age.

It has been estimated that in this country alone there are possibly two million people suffering from incontinence. A number of these, finding no help elsewhere for one reason or another, write to the Disabled Living Foundation. Any publicity such as a mention in a women's magazine brings in a spate of letters revealing problems which have often existed for years. Is it surprising that incontinence is regarded with dismay? Its consequences are unpleasant and difficult to hide, and it disturbs our senses as well as our feelings about personal privacy. It is natural that people try to

1

conceal it, even though this may make treatment impossible.

Much incontinence could be prevented by a wider dissemination of knowledge, not only about its physical aspects but also its emotional and social implications.

Causes of incontinence can be diagnosed and treated in a variety of ways by the medical profession; as well as the family doctor there are specialists concerned with the subject. Those who have this problem need to understand their own type of incontinence since, as will be explained in later chapters of this book, there are often ways in which they can help themselves either to maintain control or to regain it. Finally, where some degree of incontinence has to be accepted, it can be managed by the use of the right equipment, but for this to be effective the special requirements of each individual need to be considered.

2

The past

Incontinence is a condition which has been known for centuries but there are few references to it in literature, medical or otherwise. The Egyptians and the Greeks recorded various treatments — one of the earliest in the Egyptian medical Papyrus Ebers, dates back to 1500 BC. References have also been found to appliances designed to prevent the involuntary passing of urine.

During the past two thousand years in Western Europe incontinence in children has had more attention than that in adults, and details of treatment for them can be found, particularly dating from the sixteenth century. One of the first English books on the diseases of children, written in 1544 by Thomas Phaer, the father of paediatrics, contained a chapter 'Of Pyssing in the Bed'. Bedwetting has been regarded as a problem in most societies including some primitive communities; many remedies have been tried, including the use and abuse of fear and punishment. Adult problems have not attracted much attention, except for those in relation to women and childbirth. In 1777 Thomas Leake, a teacher of midwifery, described two devices for the prevention of incontinence, otherwise there is little recorded.

There are several possible reasons for this. Perhaps under the living conditions of the past incontinence did not present a problem: in Europe during the Middle Ages, and even much later, standards of domestic hygiene were very low; the streets were unpaved and accumulations of human as well as animal excrement produced odours which would be found unacceptable today; underclothing did not exist and bedding consisted of disposable straw. Under these conditions, the effects of incontinence would have passed unnoticed.

The development of higher standards of social and domestic hygiene and cleanliness has unfortunately been accompanied by taboos and inhibitions connected with bodily functions. Britain

3

and the United States have fared the worst in this respect, the Americans being even more prudish than ourselves with their emphasis on 'sterile' lavatories and silent flushing systems.

In this atmosphere of secrecy an incontinent person can only feel shame and embarrassment. Freud wrote in his 'Introductory Essays on Psychoanalysis' that the child feels no disgust for its own excreta until this is inculcated by the parents. By comparing one culture with another it can be seen that this feeling of embarrassment can be artificially engendered by social attitudes. In Hindu society it is polite to ask a guest about the state of his bowels, while in this country such a remark would be unthinkable. Our embarrassment is shown by the number of words we use to describe the room where these functions are performed: lavatory, water closet, WC, toilet, littlest room, powder room, ladies' room and many others.

Until lately incontinence did not receive much attention from the medical profession. Perhaps the existence of it was not divulged to the doctor, as is sometimes still the case today; also in itself it is not lethal and in most cases can be endured. However attitudes are gradually changing. Incontinence should not be allowed to make people feel social outcasts and even to separate them from their families. The admission of an elderly person to hospital because of incontinence might in some cases have been avoided by timely advice and help. With the number of elderly in the population increasing there is a great need for preventative action. Yet incontinence is a word which is rarely heard; few people talk about it and there is seldom an article in the press or a radio or television programme on the subject; it is still taboo. Many more medical people are now actively involved in developing methods of investigation and treatment, but a greater acceptance by society of the widespread existence of incontinence would help both those who have to endure it and those who are attempting to find remedies.

3

Types of incontinence

Incontinence may be urinary (connected with the bladder) or faecal (connected with the bowels).

URINARY INCONTINENCE

This is by far the most common. It may be helpful to describe the workings of the bladder and the way in which control is acquired in early life.

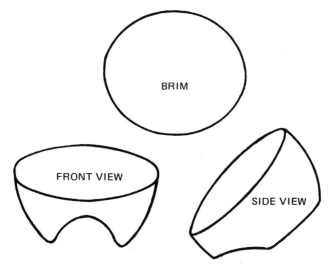

DIAGRAM 1.   BONY PELVIC BASIN

The bladder lies in the pelvis, a bony basin situated at the lower part of the spine. There is no bony wall in part of the front and no bone at the base. The basin is tilted forwards.

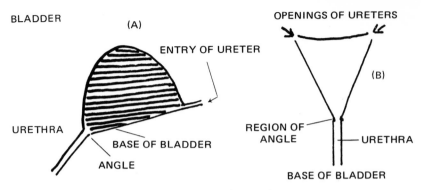

DIAGRAM 2. (A and B)

The bladder is a thin walled muscular sac with an outlet tube called the urethra. It is the reservoir for the collection of urine and can be distended to contain one pint or more of urine. Urine is carried to the bladder from the kidneys by two tubes (ureters) the ends of which pass obliquely through the muscular bladder wall and open into the base of the bladder (trigone). The urethra leads out of the front of the base at an angle; this angle functions as a valve keeping the urethra closed except during the process of passing water (micturition).

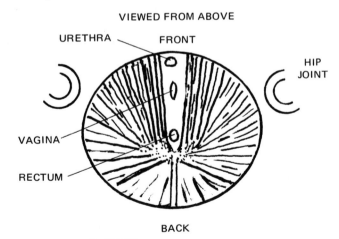

URETHRA	=	URINE PASSAGE
VAGINA	=	FRONT PASSAGE
RECTUM	=	BACK PASSAGE

DIAGRAM 3.   MUSCULAR FLOOR OF PELVIS. FEMALE.

SIDE VIEW OF PELVIS WITH BLADDER,
WOMB, BOWEL AND LEVEL OF PELVIC
MUSCLES THROUGH WHICH THEIR EXIT
TUBES PASS.

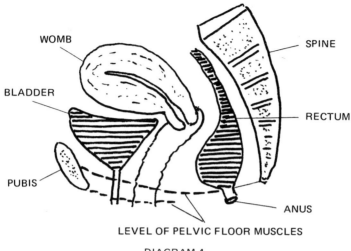

WOMB

SPINE

BLADDER

RECTUM

PUBIS

ANUS

LEVEL OF PELVIC FLOOR MUSCLES

DIAGRAM 4.

Like other organs within the pelvis (diagrams 3 & 4) the bladder
is supported by a floor consisting of two flat muscles. There is a
gap between them in front through which the exit tubes of the
organs pass. The edges of the gap can be brought together by conscious tightening and in so doing stop the passage of urine or faeces
(see exercises, p. 21). This is helped by a superficial but smaller
layer of muscle, and both play a part in maintaining continence.
Passing water is such an ordinary act that we take it for granted,
but in fact it is quite a complicated process.

Control of the bladder

In an infant before it is trained, the bladder acts automatically.
Emptying occurs as soon as the urine within the bladder reaches a
certain volume, the accompanying rise in pressure resulting in contractions of the bladder which expel the urine. This is a spon-
taneous and unconscious act controlled by a centre in the spinal
cord. As the small child develops, control from the brain is gradually established, making it possible for the voiding of urine to be
postponed. With guidance from the mother, the child learns to

pass water only in suitable places and also to go at convenient times even in the absence of any urge. This training may take up to two years or more, and everyone recognises that children frequently have accidents during this period, for instance when they are totally preoccupied in play.

Some adults having failed to develop control of the bladder in childhood continue to wet the bed (adult enuresis).

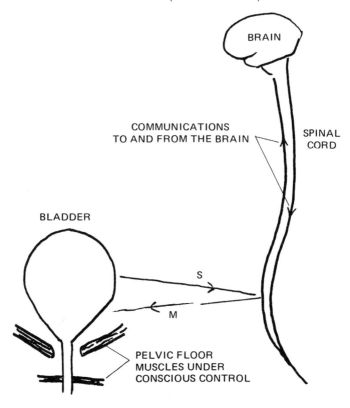

S = UNCONSCIOUS SENSATIONS FROM BLADDER TO SPINAL CORD
M = UNCONSCIOUS MESSAGES FROM SPINAL CORD TO BLADDER
BRAIN CONTROL BECOMES ESTABLISHED AS CHILD 'GROWS UP'.

DIAGRAM 5.

Natural variations

Following childhood, complete urinary control is achieved by most people but individual habits of urination vary greatly. Some pass water more frequently than others. Children, rather than use the school lavatories, learn to control their bladders until they arrive home, often holding on to a large volume of urine in the process. Some people, indeed most elderly people, need to get up in the night — the chamber pot, now seldom seen, certainly had its uses.

What can go wrong?

There are many different causes of incontinence. These include temporary illness, childbirth, local conditions affecting the bladder or womb (some forms of prolapse), complication of the arteries, and injury or disease of the spinal cord. Incontinence may take various forms, depending on the cause, so it is important to define the nature of the leakage as this can give a clue to the underlying problem.

Types of leakage

The following will be described:
(a) Stress incontinence.
(b) Urge incontinence — urgency, frequency, precipitancy.
(c) Dribbling.

Stress incontinence

In this condition urine leaks out during some slight exertion such as a cough or sneeze, and in some women even when walking or turning in bed. The main reason for this is the overstretching and laxity of the supporting structures around the urethra (bladder neck) and the weakness of the muscles of the pelvic floor. Both contribute to keeping the urethra closed. This frequently follows childbirth, though women who have not had children can be affected. As long as the leakage is small it does not present a major problem. However, the condition is likely to become more troublesome as the years pass, if no action is taken. Unfortunately many women accept it as an inevitable aftermath of childbirth; they do not mention it to the doctor and it is often not recognised at postnatal examinations. This form of incontinence is estimated to affect 30 to 40% of all women at some period in their lives. Nowadays most women are taught pelvic floor exercises after having a baby, and these, if practised conscientiously at the time, do much to prevent stress incontinence developing; for this reason effective post-natal teaching is of paramount importance.

Urge incontinence

Urgency: a wish to pass water at once, which if not satisfied may lead to incontinence. It is often accompanied by the need to pass water frequently (increased frequency).
Precipitancy: this is similar to urgency, except that there is no warning time; as soon as the desire to pass water is felt, urine pours out.

Urgency and frequency are symptoms of the irritability of the muscle of the bladder and can be caused by a urinary infection (cystitis) or other irritation of the lining of the bladder.

These symptoms, together with precipitancy, can also develop gradually as a result of decreasing control of the bladder from the brain centre. They may follow an injury to the brain, a stroke or disease of the blood vessels in the brain. They may also be caused by pressure around the outlet of the bladder as in enlargement of the prostate gland in men.

Dribbling

This term is used when urine flows away in drops or in a trickling stream. There are many causes. In men it is commonly associated with enlargement of the prostate gland, which is situated beneath the bladder neck and around the upper part of the urethra. This condition may cause complete or partial obstruction to the flow of urine from the bladder. If the bladder cannot be emptied spontaneously it gradually fills; this is known as *retention of urine*. In some cases the obstruction is incomplete, and although the bladder is never able to empty itself, small amounts of urine may constantly dribble away from the urethra. This is called *retention with overflow*. Severe constipation, by producing pressure on the urethra from the outside can have the same effect, as can uterine fibroids in women. Dribbling may also occur as the result of spinal cord diseases producing interference with the nerves which control the muscles involved in emptying the bladder.

Other factors
There are emotional and physical factors which while not connected with urinary function may result in incontinence.

Emotional factors

Emotion can affect the action of the bladder. It is quite common to feel the desire to pass water when under some temporary strain, for example before an important interview, or when frightened. In an adult an emotional shock such as bereavement may produce an episode of incontinence.

Emotional wellbeing plays a part in the complicated mechanism of continence. If an elderly person is leading a lonely life, hopelessness and apathy may lead to inactivity, immobility and the occurrence of 'accidents'. Forgetfulness and mild confusion can also upset normal habits. Admission to a strange environment like a hospital, and dependence on others for bodily needs may cause unhappiness and have a similar effect. Some doctors think that severe distress can in itself be a cause of the breakdown of the patterns of a lifetime, resulting in an inability to perform bodily functions in the accustomed places, with consequent wetting and soiling. This behaviour is not deliberate, and requires patience and understanding. On the other hand someone who has been incontinent during a period of difficulty or loneliness at home may regain control in hospital.

A word is needed about the emotional effects of incontinence on the sufferer. These can be devastating and lead to bizarre behaviour. Some people try pathetically to conceal wet or soiled pads or clothing in an attempt to deny the problem. This may seem a 'dirty' habit but it is in fact a call for help.

Physical disabilities

Arthritis may result in difficult and slow walking; if there is an urgent need to urinate and the toilet is not reached in time, incontinence will follow. Any disability of the hands and arms and, in a woman, inability to bend at the hips, may aggravate the situation. These factors have to be taken into account when planning the management of incontinence (see chapter 4).

Medicines

If confusion and drowsiness are produced by sedatives or tranquillisers incontinence may result. Diuretics (water pills) which cause the kidneys to produce more urine may give rise to urgency and frequency.

FAECAL INCONTINENCE

The process of digestion and absorption is constantly going on and
the intestines are continuously propelling their contents onward
towards the rectum (last part of the bowel) for the final discharge

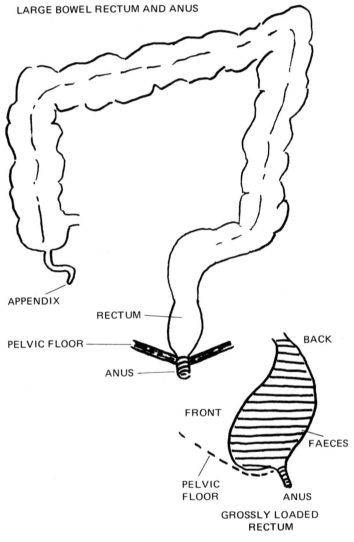

LARGE BOWEL RECTUM AND ANUS

APPENDIX

RECTUM

PELVIC FLOOR

ANUS

BACK

FRONT

FAECES

PELVIC
FLOOR

ANUS

GROSSLY LOADED
RECTUM

DIAGRAM 6.

of any unabsorbed residue. For most of the time the rectum is not loaded. (Diagram 6)

Following some habitual stimulus the contents of the large bowel are passed along to the rectum which now becomes distended with faeces. When a certain degree of distension is reached, the rectum as a whole starts to contract and empty itself. Passage of a motion can be prevented and voluntarily controlled by the contraction of the pelvic floor muscles together with the ring like muscle around the external opening of the bowel (anus). Contraction of these muscles allows the rectum to dilate and retain faeces for varying lengths of time.

A long standing accumulation of faeces in the rectum can produce one type of faecal incontinence which takes the form of liquid discharge which seeps past the impacted mass. It is sometimes known as 'overflow' diarrhoea, and is not uncommon in the elderly and inactive. A mass of faeces by producing pressure on the urethra from the outside can obstruct the flow of urine and lead also to urinary incontinence as previously mentioned.

Damage to the anal sphincter during childbirth or surgery may result in faecal incontinence. It may also occur if sphincteric control is lost due to coma, illness, nervous disease or spinal injury.

Natural variations

While a regular daily bowel action may be desirable, there is great individual variation. A survey has shown that while the normal habit for some may be three times a day, for others it may be three times a week. It is therefore important to know an individual's normal habit, and the conditions necessary to maintain it, such as time of day when a motion is passed, pattern of exercise, diet, drinking habits, etc. It is common knowledge that holidays or other environmental changes can upset such a routine; in fact any change of life style or an emotional upset may alter it.

Double incontinence

This term is used to describe a condition both urinary and faecal incontinence co-existing together and frequently inter-related.

4

Management of incontinence

Importance of attitude

We are accustomed to being able to manage those bodily functions which are under our voluntary control and it is distressing when that control is lost. Incontinence is therefore an embarrassing subject and it is often necessary to dispel the emotion-charged atmosphere which accompanies the condition. In the first place a sympathetic approach on the part of the relative, nurse or attendant is essential, to help the affected person overcome any feelings of shame. This is not easy, as in our civilised society the waste products of the body (excreta) tend to be regarded as unpleasant or even disgusting. Incontinence may arouse feelings of hostility in those who have to care for the incontinent person, possibly because of the apparent hopelessness of ever resolving or improving the condition. Professional help and advice, and moral support for the relative, can transform this situation and consequently improve relationships. A matter-of-fact attitude is reassuring since the incontinent person may be anxious not only about soiling himself but about giving trouble to others as a result. Once the confidence of the sufferer is gained the aim of further management is to enable him to cope with his disability and become as independent as possible.

URINARY INCONTINENCE

It is important first to determine the nature of the incontinence. Initially a visit to the family doctor is essential. It will help him if you are able to answer the following questions:

1. When did the trouble first develop?
2. Was the onset sudden or did it come on gradually?

3. How frequently does it occur?
4. Does it occur during the day, night or both?
5. How much urine is passed — a little or a lot?
6. What warning, if any, is received?

As explained in the last chapter, in addition it is helpful to know the kind of leakage:

1. Is there a small amount of urine which leaks out after some exertion? (stress incontinence)
2. If there is an urgent wish to pass urine, does a leakage occur unless the bladder is emptied immediately? (urge incontinence)
3. Does the passage of urine occur simultaneously with the urge to pass water? (precipitancy)
4. Is there constant dribbling with little or no awareness of wanting to pass water?

After discussion, the family doctor may wish to refer you to a specialist or centre for further investigation.

Stress incontinence:

In the early stages, especially soon after childbirth, a course of exercises to strengthen the pelvic floor muscles (which support the bladder) may be all that is required, but where there is considerable weakness of these muscles surgical treatment may be needed. Some simple self-explanatory instructions to strengthen the pelvic floor are given at the end of this chapter. Further information and details of these can be found in a useful book called 'Regaining Bladder Control'. (See Books for Further Reading Appendix C.)

NOTE: Exercising the pelvic floor muscles will also help other types of incontinence, including faecal incontinence.

Urgency:

If this occurs suddenly, it may be due to an infection or some other cause of irritation in the bladder, and a doctor should be consulted. If the onset has been gradual, as happens with some elderly people, the following suggestions may be tried:

1. If the lavatory is too far away to be reached in time, a commode can be kept by the bedside or in the living room. There

are some types made to look like ordinary fireside chairs.
(See Chapter 5).

2. For those who cannot manage to use a commode, a bedpan
   or urinal may be useful (see Chapter 5).

3. The bladder should be emptied as completely as possible at
   the time of urination. This is made easier by bending forward
   from the waist while in a sitting position with both feet on
   the floor. Using a lavatory or commode has advantage over
   using a bedpan, as long as there is no risk of overbalancing.

4. Urine should be passed at regular intervals, whether or not
   the need is felt. The bladder often learns to respond to a
   routine; a two-hour pattern suits most people. To jog the
   memory, an alarm clock or kitchen timer can be set. If the
   bladder requires emptying more frequently than every two
   hours, bladder drill (Chapter 4) may be helpful.

5. The patient should not cut down on the fluids he drinks but
   it is sensible to have more in the earlier part of the day.

6. Constipation should be avoided. Regular bowel habits are
   helped by drinking plenty of fluids, eating vegetables, fruit
   and wholemeal cereals or bran. Sometimes a glass of warm
   water in the morning or evening may stimulate the action of
   the bowel.

7. If the patient thinks that the medicines prescribed by his doctor may be the cause of losing control, especially at night, he
   should not hesitate to talk this over with him.

8. Clothes should be chosen and adapted so that they are easier
   and quicker to manage, e.g. a wrapover skirt opening at the
   back or specially adapted trousers (see Chapter 7).

9. There are circumstances in which incontinence of urine cannot be completely controlled. However, there are means of
   protection which help to maintain comfort and the ability to
   lead a normal life. (See Chapter 6).

Disabilities

If there are added physical disabilities such as arthritis here are
some suggestions which may help to increase mobility:

1. A raised lavatory seat (see p. 29) can make getting up and
   down easier, and a suitably placed grab rail can also help.

2. The toilet roll should be well placed, especially if there is any

impairment in the use of the hands, or if only one hand is usable. The interleaved type of boxed paper can be easier to manage, and soft paper is more cleansing and less likely to cause soreness.

3. A heated lavatory is an asset, especially if frequent visits are required. Any obstacles on the way to the lavatory should be removed, but where this is not possible an assessment of the time needed to get round them should be made, and allowance made accordingly. (In hospital practice it has been calculated that no-one should be more than 30 to 40 feet away from a lavatory.)

4. For someone in a wheelchair who uses a commode, the height of each should be the same to enable easy transfer from one to the other.

5. The electric switch in the lavatory should be easy to reach and so should the chain for the cistern.

Dribbling

If this form of leakage is due to constipation, the cause can easily be confirmed by the doctor or nurse and corrected by the use of enema or suppository. If a regular bowel action is thereafter ensured (see previous notes on constipation) the incontinence should not return. There are other causes of this type of incontinence, however, and the advice of the family doctor is essential as surgery or medical care may be required. If the dribbling is slight and persistent it can be contained by a device or pad.

Specialised treatment — urinary diversion

In a few rare conditions where incontinence cannot be controlled in any other way surgical treatment may be required. This may be in the form of a urinary diversion whereby the urine, instead of flowing into the bladder, is diverted to an artificial opening (stoma) on the wall of the abdomen and is collected in a bag, or the ureters are transplanted into the bowel to drain through the rectum.

Spinal injuries

In many of these the bladder can be retrained, and this training is already available at certain centres devoted to spinal injuries. (Information can be obtained from the Spinal Injuries Association

— see Appendix D.) Where bladder sensation is lost it may be possible to stimulate reflex emptying at regular intervals by tapping, kneading or stroking the lower abdomen. Where the bladder is incapable of muscular contractions hand pressure can be used to help emptying. The emptying of the bladder may be incomplete, and in some centres instruction is given in intermittent self-catheterisation. The patient is taught how to insert a soft tube (catheter) through the urethral passageway into the bladder to drain away residual urine, after which it is withdrawn. Naturally this should only be done in the first instance under medical supervision. For men with uncontrollable urinary incontinence there are urinary appliances which can be fitted to the body; the advice of a surgical appliance expert is required to ensure fit and comfort. For women there are pads and pants. (See Chapter 6).

FAECAL INCONTINENCE

The results of this may be more unpleasant than those of urinary incontinence, but a bowel motion occurs less frequently than the need to pass water. Attention to possible causes and positive management may help to prevent it, or at least make control more possible:

1. 'Overflow' diarrhoea due to constipation can be treated, and should be capable of prevention.
2. Persistent diarrhoea can arise from a number of different causes, and medical advice is essential.
3. Physical management can be made easier by the use of disposable pads and protective clothing. (See Chapter 6.)

Specialised treatment — colostomy and ileostomy

In a very few cases where faecal incontinence is due to disease or impairment of the bowel, surgery may be used to create an artificial opening (stoma) to enable the contents of the bowel to be expelled through the wall of the abdomen. This operation is called an ileostomy or colostomy, according to the position of the opening. Specialised management is necessary, involving diet, training in control, collection appliances, protective devices, etc., and in all these matters the hospital, and later the family doctor and the District (Home) Nurse, will give instruction and advice. There are also two very active self-help welfare groups. (See Appendix D.) Both give much practical guidance, as well as valuable support and encouragement. Some hospitals have stoma clinics where advice is given before and after the operation.

Spinal injury

For those with no sensation in the anal region due to injury of the spinal nerves, it is possible to establish a bowel rhythm. This involves inducing a state of mild constipation and stimulating bowel activity at planned times. This can be effected by dietary control, but suppositories and manual removal of stools may be required. This routine should be decided upon in conjunction with professional advisers.

MULTIPLE SCLEROSIS (DISSEMINATED SCLEROSIS)

In this condition there are a number of symptoms, but one of the most awkward to cope with is incontinence. By the very nature of the disease, accompanying urinary symptoms are diverse. Even the name 'multiple' reflects this. Urgency, increased frequency, and precipitancy may occur, lasting perhaps a few weeks, or months or years. In some patients acute retention of urine may be an initial problem, as the sensation of the bladder being full is impaired. The raised pressure in the distended bladder may force small amounts of urine out at intervals causing dribbling (overflow incontinence). Loss of tone in the sphincter muscles may also lead to lack of control.

Individuals differ, but the following general suggestions may prove useful:

1. Quick and easy access to the lavatory or commode is important; leave the lavatory door open.
2. Make regular visits to the toilet e.g. at 2-hourly intervals through the day, or plan visits according to the time and amount of fluid taken. The short supply of accessible public lavatories for the disabled remains a problem, but when planning social activities it is advisable to check on availability and accessibility. (A list of accessible public lavatories is available from the Central Council for the Disabled.)
3. Sanitary pads may afford sufficient protection to women where there is only minor leakage, especially if worn with

protective sani-briefs, but a pad which 'gels' when wet, and also contains a deodorant, gives especially good protection. (See Appendix B.) These may be obtainable through a local clinic.

4. Where leakage is greater, Kanga Pants (see Appendix B) are comfortable to wear, for both men and women.
5. Men can wear a urinary device, but it must be fitted by an appliance expert. It is not satisfactory to order or purchase one over the counter.
6. If retention occurs, a little pressure with the fingers on the bladder can sometimes cause urination to begin.
7. If there is persistent overflow incontinence, drainage of the bladder by catheter may be required; this is a medical decision.
8. Easily managed clothing is important, allowing for ease and speed of action. There are specially designed trousers for men with a long fly to facilitate the use of a bottle. See Chapter 7 for this and other ideas. One solution from a wheelchair user is the wearing of a kilt!

STROKE

Incontinence frequently accompanies the early phase of a stroke but is not necessarily lasting. Certain mechanical difficulties can arise, however, and these may lead to accidents, but if they are understood help can be given so that continence is maintained.

First, it is well to remember that while the patient may not be able to speak clearly or express himself he is usually very much aware of what is going on, and particularly concerned about bladder and bowel control. Activity needs to be directed to restoring independence in this respect, bearing in mind the following points:

1. As one side of the body tends to be affected it is more difficult to manage in the lavatory, or to handle a bottle or urinal, using only one hand. A technique worked out with the help of a relative or therapist will not only solve the practical problem but will also help to restore confidence. The right kind of clothing (see Chapter 7) can contribute greatly to ease of management.
2. There may be an added difficulty if the patient, when given the bottle, does not know what to do with it. Sometimes recognition of an object either by sight or touch is lost, but if

he is shown repeatedly how to use it the action will soon be re-learned.

3. Where loss of speech makes communication of bodily needs difficult, a system needs to be worked out — perhaps the ringing of a hand-bell when the need to urinate is felt.

It is not possible to know what degree of function can be restored in any particular individual, but every effort should be made to encourage independence especially in relation to bladder and bowel activity. Dependence on others for these needs is demoralising, but with patient help and the retraining of certain actions there will usually be a definite improvement.

Adult enuresis

This is not an uncommon problem. There are a number of causes, both physical and emotional, and the condition requires full medical investigation. Unfortunately through understandable embarrassment many people fail to seek advice and do not receive any adequate treatment for this distressing condition. It must be admitted that sometimes there is no simple solution, but frank discussion with the family doctor is the first step. Specialised investigation is available at centres in some areas, and the Incontinence Adviser at the Disabled Living Foundation can give advice and information.

WAYS OF IMPROVING CONTROL

Exercises for pelvic muscles

In some cases of urinary incontinence a great deal can be done to improve the condition by the use of simple physical techniques carried out by the individual.

The following instructions for strengthening the pelvic muscles in the treatment of stress incontinence have been evolved by a physiotherapist and are most effective if carried out conscientiously over a period of at least three months. Improvement will be gradual so patience and perseverance are essential.

1. Sit, stand or lie comfortably, without tensing the muscles of the seat, abdomen or legs, and pretend you are trying to control diarrhoea by tightening the ring of muscle round the back passage. Do this several times until you feel certain that

you have identified the area and are making the correct movement.

2. Sit on the lavatory or commode and commence to pass water, and while doing so make an attempt to stop the flow in midstream by contracting the muscles round the front passage. Do this also several times until you feel sure of the movement, and of the sensation of applying conscious control.

3. Exercise as follows: sitting, standing or lying, tighten first the back passage muscles and then the front, and then both together. Count four slowly, and then release the muscles. Do this four times, repeating the whole sequence once every hour if possible. With practice the movements should be quite easy to master and the exercises can be carried out at any time — while waiting for a bus, standing at the sink, watching television or lying comfortably in bed.

Remember that these must be carried out daily for at least two to three months as frequently as possible.

Bladder drill

A simple form of bladder drill may be practised to diminish frequency. Whenever passing urine, the flow should be deliberately stopped and then started again; this is a means of control which can be recognised and made use of. Then an attempt should be made, by 'holding on' in this way, to wait a little longer before passing urine the next time; this interval should gradually be lengthened, step by step, day by day. It takes time to train the bladder and patience is required, but for example hourly visits to the lavatory to pass urine may eventually be extended to twohourly. This positive and practical action which the individual can try for himself is of great value especially when frequency is caused by anxiety.

5

Aids to continence and hygiene

There are a number of items of equipment which can be of great use in the management of incontinence, especially if disability makes movement slow and difficult.

Urinal

This is a receptacle into which urine can be passed, and as it can be kept nearby it is particularly useful for someone with urgency and very little warning time; it is also useful for someone who cannot move easily.

Male urinals

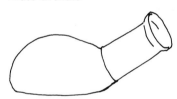

This is an example of a conventional male urinal commonly known as a bottle. There are many different makes, some in lightweight plastic (polypropylene),

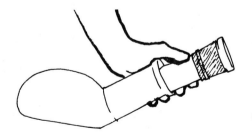

and others in glass or stainless steel. A bottle can be fitted with a non-spill adaptor to prevent spilling in the bed or chair.

There is also a disposable plastic collector with a built-in non-returnable valve. These pack flat and are sold in boxes of 10, and would be very useful when travelling or on holiday.

Female urinals

Apart from the familiar type of bedpan used in hospitals by both men and women there are urinals and bedpans especially designed for women.

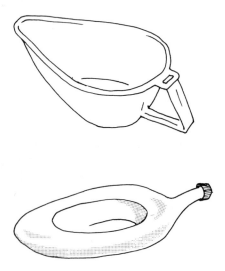

St. Peter's Boat is a pointed dish with handle which can be slipped easily between the legs and can be used while standing or sitting.

Another type is a small shallow dish with an inward-curving splash-proof rim and a capped hollow handle through which it can be emptied. This dish can be slipped under the buttocks without having to raise the hips, and is small enough to manage with one hand.

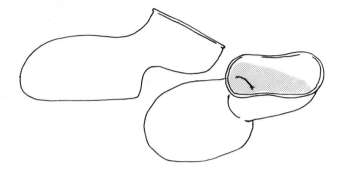

The swan-type urinal is similar to the male bottle, but with a wider neck; it is specially shaped to be held close to the body.

A fracture bedpan is wedge-shaped and designed to be slipped under the body without raising the pelvis. It can be used in a semi-recumbent position.

A device of particular use when travelling can be made at home from a soft plastic funnel with a short length of flexible tubing attached; this can empty into a hot water bottle (which can be closed and emptied unobtrusively later). The non-spill disposable plastic container already described could also be used for this.

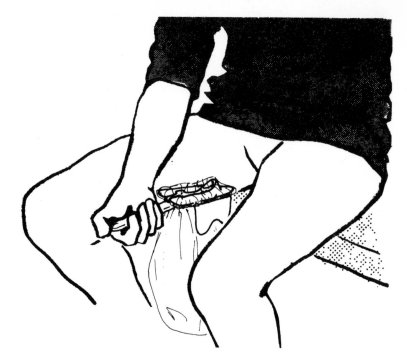

A new type of urinal has just become available, designed by a research nurse. It consists of a moulded plastic section, contoured to fit the female body, with a short handle in front by means of which it can be held comfortably and firmly in position. A disposable plastic bag with an elasticated top fits over the rim of the device and is suspended from it to collect the urine. It can be used while sitting, standing or lying down, and it is possible to stand it down quite safely after use without risk of spilling as the moulded section has straight sides. The bag can be emptied, disposed of or if necessary reused. The urinal is small and light and could be carried in a handbag.

Commodes

If the lavatory is far away, upstairs or outside, a commode or a chemical closet can be used instead. Commodes can be kept either in the bedroom or the living room, and some are designed to look like ordinary fireside chairs. In choosing a commode, the following points need to be taken into account:

1. It is important that it should be the right height for the user to sit comfortably, with both feet firmly on the floor.
2. It should have a firm base with its legs wider than its arms. One with arms and a back rest is usually best, but where the user needs to transfer from bed or wheelchair there are types with swinging or removable arms.
3. If the commode needs to be moved, it should have castors or wheels which can be braked when it is in use.
4. A sani-chair may be appropriate; this is a lavatory seat set in a chair-frame on wheels, so that the user can be wheeled, or can propel himself, over a lavatory or commode. Before acquiring one of these, the height of the lavatory or commode must be checked to make sure that the sani-chair will go over it.

Cushions

For someone who is unable to move and who spends long periods alone the Easinurse Cushion or the Paraplegic Cushion may be useful. These are specially designed with openings or removable sections to accommodate a bedpan or other receptacles. They do, how-

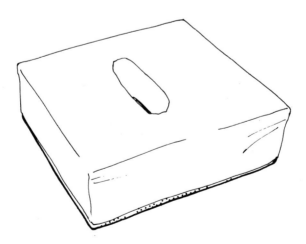

ever, have certain disadvantages — not everyone finds it easy to sit in the correct position, and some users may find them uncomfortable. There is also an Easinurse mattress which is similar in principle for someone confined to bed, but this may not always be convenient.

Chemical closets

A portable lavatory of the kind used when camping or caravanning may sometimes be preferable, as it does not have to be emptied immediately. There are a number of different models, including some with a limited flushing system. Size and stability should be considered as well as capacity; the smaller the model the lighter it will be to empty, but for a heavy or disabled user a small closet may need to be placed in a firm-based frame.

Aids in the lavatory

If the lavatory can be reached there are various ways of making it more comfortable and easier to use. The following suggestions may be helpful:

1. Access should be made as easy as possible, and any obstacles removed. If there is insufficient room to manoeuvre inside, perhaps the door could be re-hung so as to open outwards.

2. If the lavatory is cold it can be heated economically by means of a low-voltage electrical tubular heater at skirting-board level. This can be left on at all times, but in the interests of safety it should be protected by a guard. Alternatively a wall heater high up on the wall could be used.

3. For those who have difficulty in bending at the hips, a raised lavatory seat makes sitting down and getting up easier. There are various types which raise the height of the seat by 4 to 6 inches. They are placed directly on top of the lavatory pan and some are adjustable to its size, as well as adjustable in height. Others can be fixed to have a tilt. They are easily removed for normal use.

Raised lavatory seat

4. Sometimes support is needed when standing or arranging clothing. A grab rail suitably placed on the lavatory wall can be a great help, but it is essential that it should be fixed securely enough to take the necessary strain, and at the best angle for the user. An alternative might be a horizontal bar fixed to one or both walls at about waist level.

Another form of horizontal support consists of a drop-down bar, fixed to the wall behind the lavatory, with a drop-down right-angled supporting leg; this has the advantage of folding back against the wall when not in use, and so gives access to wheel chair users. There are also chrome rails which are designed to close across the front of the user, to give all round support to the frail or unsteady. This support is locked in place through the mounting holes of the lavatory seat, and the enclosing arms swing back out of the way for getting on and off the lavatory.

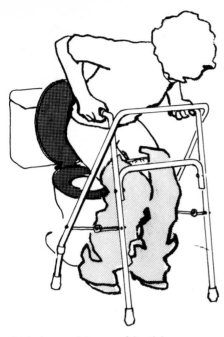

5. Some walking frames are of a design to fit across the lavatory and provide support getting on and off.
6. It is important the toilet paper should be placed so that it can be reached without difficulty, especially if there is restricted use of one arm or hand. A box of interleaved paper or paper handkerchief tissues may be easier to manage than a toilet roll. All toilet paper should be soft for maximum efficiency of action.

Aids in washing and bathing

1. Cleansing and washing while sitting on the lavatory itself can be made easier by the fitting of a horse-shoe shaped lavatory seat with a front opening. A portable bidet is another useful device; this is a shallow plastic bowl which can be slipped under the user to rest on the top of the lavatory pan. It is filled with warm water from a jug (or by hose from a nearby tap) and empties straight into the lavatory through a plug-hole.

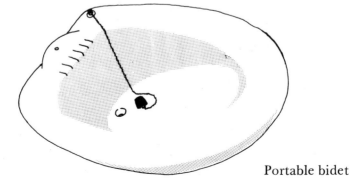

Portable bidet

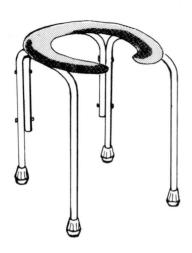

2. A shower stool with a horseshoe shaped seat may be a solution for those who need to wash or shower sitting down. It can be used in the shower stall, or standing in the bath in conjunction with a shower hose, but even by itself it provides a good well-supported position for an all-over wash. There are many types of shower seats, some with arm and back supports, and some on wheels.

3. If the bath can be used there are hoists to assist in lifting the disabled person. There are special seats which can be fitted into the bath to make it easier to get in and out. A board fitted across the top of the bath makes it possible for someone who cannot stand to transfer from chair to bath. A shower hose bought from the chemist and fitted to the taps may make washing easier.

Useful aids found in some hospitals

1. There are lavatories which incorporate an automatic warm water douche and a warm air duct for drying. They can be operated by foot or by a variety of hand or arm controls. One type requires sophisticated plumbing and skilled installation, as well as first class maintenance. The other is an adaptation of a standard lavatory.
2. There are now washing machines on the market which combine sluicing and washing. They require no special plumbing and can be used in wards where incontinence is a problem so that patients' own clothing can be laundered quickly and conveniently. They would undoubtedly be equally useful in residential homes where the same problems are found.

Appendix A

Urinals etc.

The District (Home) Nurse may help with the provision of this kind of equipment. It can also be bought or ordered from many large chemists and surgical suppliers. The range is wide, but the following details of manufacturers or distributors may be useful:

Capecraft Ltd.
The Cape
Warwick CV34 5DL
(Plastic urinals, St. Peter's Boat)

Downs Surgical Ltd.
Church Path
Mitcham, Surrey
(Reddy-Bottle: disposable flat-pack urine collector)

Searle Medical
PO Box 88, Lincoln Road
High Wycombe, Bucks
HP12 3RE
(A newly developed female device, with suspended plastic bag)

William Freeman and Co. Ltd.
Suba-Seal Works
Staincross, Barnsley
(Plastics, including dish urinal with hollow handle)

Chas. F. Thackray Ltd.
PO Box 171, Park Street
Leeds LS1 1RG
(Glass urinals, non-spill adaptor)

TLF Pland Ltd.
Lower Wortley Ring Road
Leeds LS12 6AA
(Stainless steel urinals)

Commodes and other aids

In many cases these are supplied through the social services department. Comprehensive descriptive lists, with details of manufacture and supply, and a guide to current prices, are kept by the Disabled Living Foundation, from whom information can be obtained. A wide variety of items is on permanent display at the DLF Aids Centre.

Hospital aids

The addresses below may be useful:

Clos-o-mat (Gt. Britain) Ltd.
2 Brooklands Road
Sale, Cheshire M33 3SS
(Lavatory requiring special plumbing)

Medic-Bath Ltd.
Ashfield Works
Hulme Hall Lane
Manchester M10 8AZ
(Medic-Loo; combined lavatory and douche)

Standrette Ltd.
Rex House
492 Merton Road
London SW18 5AE
(Rex Hygeian Sluice-and-Wash)

6

Protective equipment

There are certain circumstances in which incontinence of urine cannot be completely controlled. However, there are means of protection which help to maintain comfort and the ability to lead a normal life; these are collection devices and various forms of pads and pants.

Male

There are a number of body worn appliances designed for men, and a complete list can be found in 'Portable Urinals and Related Equipment'. (See Books for Further Reading – Appendix C.) It is essential to have advice from an expert fitter, as each individual may require a different type or size. These appliances fit on to the penis, and some enclose the scrotum as well. Urine is collected in a bag strapped to the leg and concealed inside the trouser leg. There are also devices for dribbling. Most hospitals have an appliance officer, and some large chemists and surgical suppliers have appliance experts and fitting rooms. (See Appendix B for addresses.) Pants and padding suitable for men are also available.

Female

There are as yet no satisfactory appliances for women to wear. In some cases the doctor may decide that an in-dwelling catheter is advisable. Usually, however, absorbent pads and protective pants are the solution. Some pants are made of plastic, some of a specially treated nylon fabric (duralite) and there is one type made of hydrophobic (one-way) fabric. There are many styles available and the following illustrations indicate those most appropriate in different circumstances.

Pull-on style, suitable for more active users.

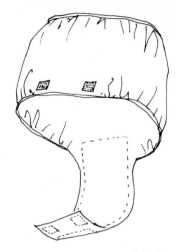

Drop-front pull-on, useful for wheelchair users. The pad can be changed without removing the pants.

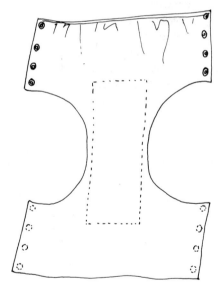

Open-flat style, easier to put on when lying flat. Also suitable for wheelchair users.

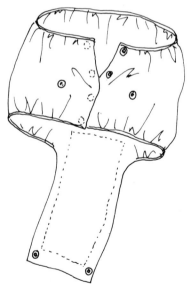

Drop-front open-flat, can be fastened at waist level, so that garment remains in place when front is dropped.

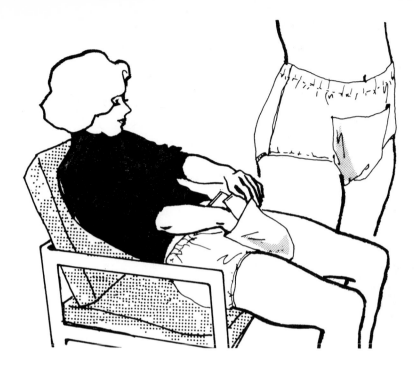

Kanga Pants are made of knitted one-way fabric through which the urine passes to be absorbed by a pad which is held in a plastic pouch on the *outside* of the garment. Provided the pad is changed regularly, the pants and the body of the wearer remain dry. The pad can be changed without removing the pants, although it is necessary to raise the body slightly to do this. A close fit is necessary and sizing is by hip measurement. There are both pull-on and open-flat drop-front styles. They are not suitable for nightwear or for double incontinence.

Disposable pants and pads

Sometimes fully disposable protection is needed, and there are some items which combine both pants and pad.

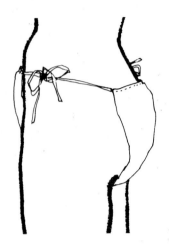

One style of adult diaper consists of a wide strip of padding which ties at the waist with tapes. It affords protection in cases of moderate leakage, and would be useful for instance on a journey.

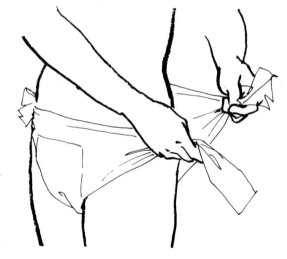

Another consists of a soft plastic bikini tying at the sides, with a highly absorbent core of cellulose pulp. It gives very good protection and can be used in cases of faecal incontinence.

Another is made in napkin style, as shown, with self-fastening patches. It combines a waterproof covering and a highly absorbent lining, and can be put on and changed easily even when the user is confined to bed or chair. This type also is particularly suitable for double incontinence. The same manufacturers also make disposable pants which can be worn over the napkin for greater security, although the size of these should be checked.

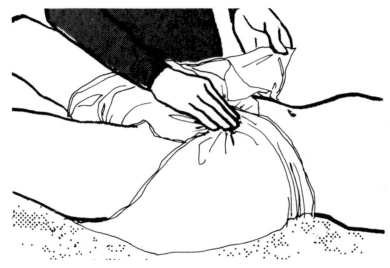

Mesh pants

There are also pants made of stretch nylon mesh which hold in place a plastic-backed pad. They stretch to fit any size wearer, and are extremely light and comfortable, but as a slight effort is required to pull them up they are perhaps more suitable for an active person or for someone with the use of both hands.

Pads

There are many different pads available. Some pants have their own special variety, either washable or disposable, and the type used will depend on the needs of the user and on how much absorption is required. Pads can be made from Inco Roll (obtainable on prescription) to any required size and thickness. The following is another way of making a pad, using materials obtainable on prescription from the family doctor.

Roll of gauze tissue 275 metres (300 yards) X 20 cm (8″)
Roll of brown *non*-absorbent cottonwool
Roll of white absorbent wool
Cellulose tissue

To make up: cut wool and cellulose to required size, then cut the gauze approximately 6″ longer. Open gauze out fully on a flat surface, making sure it is free from creases; place brown wool, cellulose and white wool, layered in that order, on to the gauze and fold the gauze over until the pad is completely enclosed; tuck the ends neatly into the layers of wool. The pad is worn with the white wool side next to the skin.

One particular pad, which looks like an ordinary sanitary pad, contains a substance which 'gels' when wet, and absorbs about three times as much fluid as an average one of similar size. It also contains a deodorant.

Ordinary sanitary pads, some of which have self-adhesive spots for attaching to pants, are useful for slight dribbling. Similarly a jock-strap type sanitary pant to which the pad is attached may be convenient.

Underpads

There are a number of types available to absorb urine and protect the bed. They have a porous surface, and under this is an absorbent material with plastic backing.

Points to consider are:

1. The top surface must be sufficiently porous, otherwise the urine will spill on the bed.

2. If the surface material irritates the skin another type must be tried.
3. Check the absorptive capacity of the pad. In circumstances where the pad cannot be changed frequently a capacity of 500 to 600 ml. (about a pint) is necessary. Some pads become saturated with much less than this. It is a common practice, especially in hospitals, to use two or three pads at a time, but this is useless and wasteful since the urine cannot pass through the plastic backing of the top pad.
4. The position of the pad is important. It should be placed across the bed under the buttocks and not lengthwise. A typical pad measures 60 cm (24″) X 40 cm (18″) but one of 75 cm (30″) X 57 cm (23″) is often more appropriate.

These are only a selection of some of the items on the market, but even as this book goes to press more are coming out, and the increasing ingenuity and adaptability of the designers and manufacturers show that the needs of the incontinent are beginning to be understood.

Appendix B

Male appliances

Firms with facilities for consultation and fitting include:

John Bell and Croyden
50 Wigmore Street, London W1

Downs Surgical Ltd.
Consulting Rooms
34 New Cavendish Street, London W1

The Genito-Urinary Manufacturing Co. Ltd.
33-34 Devonshire Street, London W1

Medical Supply Association
King's Cross Road
Dundee DD2 3QE

Pryor and Howard Ltd.
Fitting Rooms
33 Birkbeck Road, London N17

Pants, pads and bedpads

The District (Home) Nurse or local clinic can supply these, though the range offered may be limited. It is, however, the responsibility of the National Health Service to provide those most appropriate to the needs of the user, so it is worth persevering in order to obtain the required items.

   Local chemists stock certain types, or will order others; in case of difficulty, or if preferred, there are mail order firms which specialise in the supply of such equipment, and these include:

Bodycare (R. and G. Associates)
3 Nails Lane, Bishops Stortford, Herts.

Home Nursing Supplies Ltd.
PO Box W4, Westbury, Wilts.

HUB Marketing Ltd.
Castle Street, Bampton, Devon EX16 9NS

The following addresses of manufacturers may also be useful:

Gelulose Incontinence Products
16 Dolphin Street
Manchester M12 6BG
(Gelulose Pad — a 'gelling' pad)

Kanga Hospital Products Ltd.
PO Box 39, Bentinck Street
Bolton, BL1 4EX
(Kanga Pants)

Molnlycke Ltd.
Sancella House
Station Approach
Harpenden, Herts.
(Tie-side bikini style, disposable adult diaper with tapes and feather-weight stretch pants)

Vernon Carus Ltd.
Penwortham Mills
Preston, Lancs.
(Cumfies — self fastening disposable napkin)

The following firms make various styles of protective pants:

Bowman Health Products
Bowman House
154 Marylebone Road, London NW1

Contenta Surgical Co.
Grove Estate, Dorchester, DT1 1SU

Henleys Ltd.
Alexandra Works
Clarendon Road, London N8

Johnson and Johnson Ltd.
Slough, Bucks.

Loxley Luxan Medical Supplies Ltd.
Bessingby Industrial Estate
Bridlington, North Humberside, YO16 4SU

Robinsons of Chesterfield
Derbyshire S40 2AD

Bedpads

These include:

Inco Underpads, manufactured by:
Robinsons of Chesterfield
Derbyshire S40 2AD

The Polyweb, manufactured by:
Smith and Nephew – Southalls Ltd.
Alum Rock Road
Birmingham, B8 3DY
(Is widely stocked, and provides good absorption)

Drawsheet

Marathon Dri-Sheet (one-way drawsheet referred to on page 57) is obtainable from local chemists or direct from:

J. H. Bounds Ltd.
Stethos House
68 Sackville Street
Manchester

Neutralising deodorant

Nilodor: obtainable from large chemists or direct from:

Loxley Luxan Medical Supplies Ltd.
Bessingby Industrial Estate
Bridlington, North Humberside, YO16 4SU

As with many other items dealt with in this book, the Disabled Living Foundation keep comprehensive lists of pads, pants, etc. and examples are displayed in the Aids Centre.

7

Clothing

It is important to all of us that we look our best, in clothes of our own choosing. To someone who is incontinent, the choice of clothing is particularly important as it not only affects appearance but can make the condition more manageable. Certain styles, easy fastenings and modern easy-care materials can facilitate this.

If there is need to pass urine in a hurry, ease of handling and quick removal or adjustment of clothing are essential. The following are some suggestions:

For women

A full skirt is easier and quicker to pull up.
A pinafore style dress without a waist seam is easier to manipulate.
Choose easy-fitting slacks with an elasticated waist.

For men

Specially designed or adapted trousers. The 'Edgware' trouser has a fly opening right down to the crutch seam, making the use of a bottle easier.

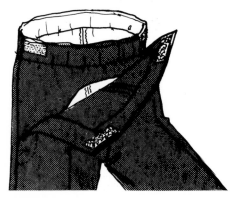

Trousers can be obtained with a drop front.

Fastenings

Easy fastenings not only aid quick action, but are helpful if there is any disability especially in the hands. Try any of the following:

Large buttons.
Toggles.
Buttons sewn on with a long shank.
Large hooks.
Longer zips, with a tab or ring to pull on.
Velcro — this is best used in small dabs as these are easier to close than long strips. The 'hooks' side of the Velcro should not be placed where it is likely to come into contact with body hair. The Velcro must be closed during laundering.

Day clothes

For someone sitting most of the day, garments which open flat and wrap around are the easiest to put on and take off, and if separates are worn the lower garment can be taken off without having to be pulled over the head.

If a man's shirt is shortened it will be more comfortable and less likely to become wet.

Other suggestions:

A wrap-round skirt worn with the opening at the back.

A skirt with a sprung clip waist-band can be slipped round the waist from the front. If a dress is preferred, a button-through style is easy to put on and can be made with an opening back panel.

The Edgware trousers already mentioned have a high back and full cut seat for comfort when sitting, wide legs and simple fastening. They are also smart, look like any other pair of trousers and at present come in five colours, in easy-care washable material. Other colours and materials will become available as demand increases.

Underclothes

Ordinary cotton pants are more comfortable than nylon.

French knickers (which are now being manufactured again) with wide legs can sometimes just be pulled aside.

Back-opening knickers are helpful in some situations, but check that the opening is large enough.

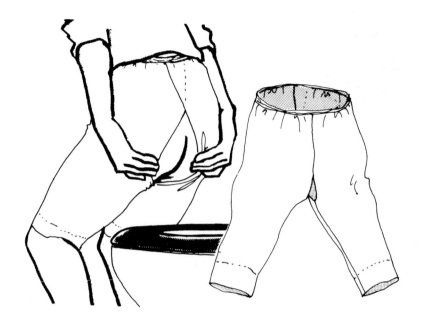

Drop-front knickers are also available, but if the drop front is difficult to retrieve and handle it may drop into the lavatory pan.

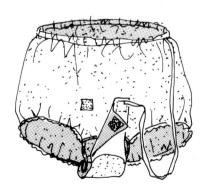

Knickers can be adapted to
open flat for someone who
cannot stand up to put
them on.

Tights are available with a divided gusset, but it is as well to
check the size of the opening.

Suspender-tights are useful. These are like long stockings right
up to the waist, kept up like tights by means of an elasticated
waistband, but open so that any kind of protective pant can be
worn with them.

A narrow suspender belt, as for maternity wear, may be more
suitable than a corset as the latter may become wet especially if
padding is worn.

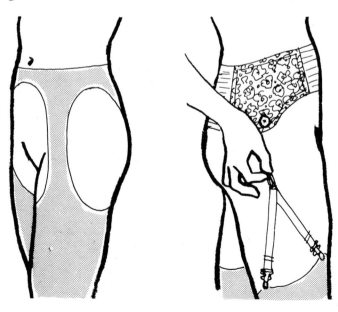

Where there is difficulty in doing up suspenders, detachable ones are useful as they can be attached to the stockings first and then to the supporting garment.

Some may like a Liberty bodice as it provides support and warmth; the short version is more suitable to wear with protective garments.

Self-supporting stockings do not require suspenders, but may cause restriction to veins.

Nightwear

A nightdress which opens in front but has a wrapover back is easy to put on and take off. If it has a good overlap it will cover the wearer when standing, but can be pulled aside when necessary.

A back opening dressing gown can be worn.

Appliances

If an appliance is worn the following suggestions may be useful:

For men

Boxer shorts or athletic trunks are best as the wide leg allows room for the appliance.

A zip fastener in the inside seam of the trouser leg allows for easy emptying and changing of the bag.

For women

If a catheter is worn, the tube can be taken down through the knicker leg. If slacks are worn, a zip can be put in the leg seam as described above for access to the bag.

Some people might like to wear a long narrow apron with a pocket to hold the bag; this can be worn under a skirt which is fairly long and full.

Aids to dressing for those with special problems

If there is paralysis of one side of the body, ways of managing with one hand have to be considered.

1. When the skirt is lifted up it can be tucked into the waist-band, or into a soft elastic worn round the waist.

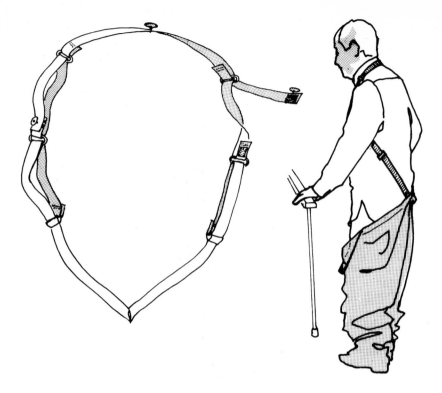

2. Special braces enable the trousers to be dropped and pulled up with one hand.
3. Pants can be attached to trousers with two or three dabs of Velcro sewn on to the outside of the waistband of the pants and the inside of the waistband of the trousers. The soft side of the Velcro must be put on the pants, as these are washed more frequently.

Materials and laundering

Washing can be made easier by the use of drip-dry fabrics for outer garments, and stretch synthetics are comfortable in wear.
    The use of separates can save washing a whole garment.

Laundry

As with bed-linen, clothing if wet or soiled should be rinsed and soaked immediately in cold water to prevent staining.

As already mentioned, in some hospitals wards have their own sluicing and washing machines so that patients can wear their own clothes, and these can be quickly laundered and returned to them.

Clothing is very important to the individual's morale, so it is always worthwhile to consider to what extent ordinary clothing can be adapted. Part of the treatment for incontinence is to manage it in such a way that normal social life can be enjoyed.

Further clothing information

The Clothing Adviser of the DLF will give general advice and information, and detailed lists of clothing suitable for the elderly and the handicapped, as well as for those affected by incontinence, with a guide to prices, are available. Examples of clothing, including that for children, are on permanent display. A book on *Dressing for Disabled People: A manual for nurses and others,* advising on dressing both aided and unaided, choice of clothes, and toileting, including aspects of incontinence, has recently been published. (See App. C.)

8

Practical hints

Personal care

Keep the skin as dry as possible by frequent changing of underpads or pads. If urine is left on the skin or clothing, it decomposes and ammonia (an alkali) is released which irritates the skin.

Wash the area with a soft cloth and ordinary soap and water before renewing the pad. A barrier cream can prevent soreness. If powder is used, use it sparingly. Washing may be difficult, especially if there is any disability. A tissue or cloth covering a foam mop may help. Sometimes special wet sealed medical tissues are helpful. A portable bidet may be useful for someone able to use the lavatory (see p. 31).

Laundry

If linen is soiled it should be rinsed out and soaked in cold water in a covered bucket. Napisan can be added to help the cleaning action. The article can then be washed in the normal way and no staining or smell should result. Biological washing powders are sometimes used but care should be taken as these are strong and may irritate the skin. A special laundry service may be available in the area. Enquire about this. (See chapter 11.)

Used disposable pads should be put in a plastic bag, inside another closed container. In this way any smell which may arise from decomposing excreta is eliminated.

Commodes

If a commode or bedpan is used it should be emptied immediately. If this is not possible, add disinfectant or neutraliser or cat litter. Any of these will help to remove the smell. A round steel bowl (Welsh hat) is easier to clean than one shaped like a bedpan.

The bed

This should be as comfortable as possible, bearing in mind that the mattress must be protected.

1. If the patient is lying on an underpad which irritates the skin, or which has sharp edges from the plastic backing, a draw sheet can be placed over it.
2. One way of making up the bed might be as follows:
   A sheet of thin plastic, which is cheap and comfortable, is placed across the mattress. A piece 1 metre by 2 m would be suitable. There are waterproof mattress covers but these tend to be hot. Next put on the bottom sheet, then a second piece of plastic the same size as the first, and then an underpad or layer of wadding. On top of this can be placed a draw sheet, or for maximum comfort a draw sheet made of a special washable one-way material. This material allows the urine to pass through to the pad without becoming wet itself, so that the skin of the patient remains dry provided the underpad is renewed frequently enough. These draw sheets are made in two sizes, 84 cm (33") × 84 cm (33"), and 84 cm (33") × 43 cm (17"), and the material can also be bought by the yard, 75 cm (30") wide. (See Appendix B.)

Odour

There are a number of neutralising deodorants which help to eliminate odour. One example in Nilodor (see p 45). A drop or two can be used in appliances, commode pans, urinals, bedpans and on protective padding. A few drops can be added to the water used for washing commodes, carpets etc.

9

Admission to hospital

A WORD TO THE PATIENT

If you are admitted to hospital for any reason, the following suggestions may be helpful:

1. Be sure to tell Sister about your individual personal needs — for example how often you need to pass water, and whether you require a commode by the bed. In some hospitals these are provided, and if you need to go often and very quickly, especially at night, try to obtain one.
2. Hospital wards are frequently large and the lavatories may be some distance away. Find out immediately where they are, and whether you can walk there; if you walk slowly, be sure to allow yourself plenty of time.
3. If you have to use a bedpan, do not be shy about asking for it. The nurse will not know your personal needs unless you tell her. Using a bedpan may be a little strange at first.
4. Most hospitals nowadays have beds of which the height can be adjusted — do not be afraid to say if your bed seems too high or too low for you to be able to get in and out comfortably and without help.
5. There may be set times for 'toilet rounds' in your wards, but your bladder may need to be emptied more frequently. Explain this to Sister.
6. Even if you are incontinent at times make sure you satisfy your thirst.
7. It takes some time to settle down in hospital, and your bowel habits may alter as they tend to do on holiday. Try if possible to keep to the same routine as when you are at home, and do not be afraid of letting the nursing staff know what it is — not everyone has a daily bowel action, and 'normal' can mean anything from three times a day to three times a week.

A WORD TO THE NURSE

As incontinence causes so much emotional distress, the attitude of the nurse, like that of the relative at home, is most important, and in fact plays a key role in treatment. Patients are frequently reticent and shy about their bodily functions. If embarrassment and anxiety (as well as unnecessary incontinence) are to be avoided, the nurse must take the initiative and introduce the subject with sympathy and tact but with a matter of fact approach. This will help to gain the confidence and trust of the patient. Once this is established reassurance should be given that the nursing staff accept any difficulties with understanding and tolerance. The nurse should bear in mind that what she may take in her stride is to the patients concerned, distasteful behaviour of which they feel deeply ashamed. She has been trained to wash and change her patients when necessary and accepts this routine duty, but for the individual the need for this may be felt as a humiliating experience.

The manner in which questions are asked is of great importance in getting truthful and informative answers. For example, a kindly and sympathetic 'Do you wet yourself?' or 'Do you have any trouble with your waterworks?' followed by 'Let's see what we can do to help improve things' never fails to get a positive response. Patients can then be asked about their normal pattern of micturition before coming into hospital, and this should be recorded in the notes so that everyone in the ward may base their management on what was done at home.

Practical aspects

1. Show patients where the lavatories are, and help them to find out how long it takes to get there.
2. Impress upon them that they must never mind asking for a bedpan or bottle, and that they should ask as soon as they feel the need, and not leave it too late. Always try to answer such requests as soon as possible, as anxiety can result in increased frequency.
3. A bedside commode might be the answer for those with urgency, especially if they are able to transfer themselves from one to the other. The bed should be the same height for ease of transfer.

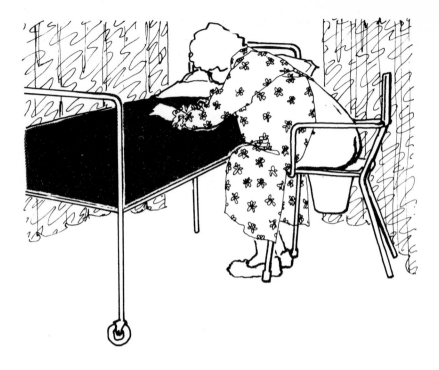

4. Make sure there is privacy. To ensure that the bladder is completely emptied, the patient should sit in a comfortable and
relaxed position. Bending forward from the waist helps, provided there is no risk of overbalancing. Sitting on a commode
which faces the side of the bed can be helpful and reassuring
to both user and attendant.
5. It does help to observe the habits of each individual patient
so that the ward routine can be planned to cater for varying
personal needs.
6. A proportion of patients in the ward may need to be re-
minded to pass water, and if necessary given assistance, every
two hours or less. Sometimes a patient may object, but with
coaxing a routine can be established and accidents avoided. It
may take a week or two.
7. The bowel routine of an individual is likely to change on
admission to hospital, and this needs to be watched to prevent

constipation. Observation of stool is important as the patient's own account may be far from accurate. The ambulant patient can be asked not to flush the lavatory after use.

10

Incontinence in children

Enuresis

This may be due to the interruption of the normal development pattern. It is called enuresis and when it happens at night, nocturnal enuresis. There may be a physical cause but it may also be due to emotional factors. On the other hand some children are just slower in developing conscious control, so no child should be labelled 'enuretic' before the age of 8 years. In some cases control is not acquired until later and some reach adulthood still with the problem of 'wetting' during the night and day.

Specific incontinence

A child born with some malformation may have a persistent leakage. A mentally retarded child may have difficulty in acquiring control or be incapable of this.

MANAGEMENT OF INCONTINENCE IN CHILDREN

Enuresis

If the child is enuretic there are special centres where the condition can be supervised and advice provided. This is not usually necessary before the age of 6 or 7 years. Parents can best help the child at all stages by encouragement rather than by punishment or reprimand.

Nocturnal enuresis (Bed-wetting)

It is advisable for the child not to have a drink near his bedtime. The parents should wake the child before retiring and encourage him to pass water. For the older child who has fully developed the awareness of bladder sensation, a waking alarm system may be tried. An electric 'buzzer' is activated as soon as a few drops of urine fall onto a special pad on which the child lies, thus waking him up. In time, this builds up a reflex and the child wakens just before he needs to urinate.

Bladder training

Bladder training is essential at all stages. The child is asked to say when he feels like urinating and is then encouraged to 'hold on' for increasing periods of time. This will diminish the frequency of night time wetting, as the capacity of the bladder is thereby increased. A chart will help both child and parent to assess progress.

Specific incontinence

Any physical handicap involving urinary problems requires specialised advice. Mentally handicapped children can often be trained to gain control over bladder and bowel action. It will take a longer period of time than for the average child, and if speech is difficult other ways of communication have to be found. Advice can be obtained from the National Society for Mentally Handicapped Children. (See Appendix D.)

Clothing

For information about clothing for the incontinent disabled child, there is a most useful publication 'Clothing for the Handicapped Child'. (See Appendix C.)

11

Services available

There are a number of services to help those who are incontinent. Unfortunately embarrassment sometimes prevents people from asking and finding out what can be done. The following is a guide to available services, though resources vary very much from one area to another.

HEALTH SERVICES

Doctor

The family doctor will supply the initial medical advice, and arrange for a visit to a specialist or specialised hospital centre if necessary.

District (Home) Nurse

If nursing advice and assistance are required, the doctor will arrange for the District Nurse to call. In some areas a Nursing Auxiliary may assist with daily bathing and dressing, and night nursing can sometimes be arranged for those patients who may require it. The District Nurse, as a member of the primary health care team, will maintain continuity of care, when necessary, between hospital and home.

Health Visitor

The Health Visitor is a nurse with additional training to enable her to advise on a number of points including health education and social needs. She can fulfil these functions when visiting disabled or elderly people in their own home. She will attempt to sort out what kind of help should be given in consultation with the patient, his family, and, if necessary, with other members of the caring team including the Social Worker.

Practical help available

The District Nurse or Health Visitor can advise about the following:

1. The supply and use of equipment, such as urinals, protective pants, pads, bedpads, etc.
2. Incontinent Laundry Service to collect soiled linen and sometimes nightclothes.
3. Disposal Service to collect soiled pads and bedpads. There may be a special collection or bags may be supplied to put out with ordinary refuse. This service is usually run by the Cleansing Department.

SOCIAL SERVICES

Social Worker

The Social Worker from the Social Services Department of the Local Authority can help with individual or family stress, and advise about practical help available. In many areas there are also occupational therapists who can give practical advice. The following services may be available:

1. Home Help: to help with housework, sometimes with laundry, and sometimes with such personal needs as washing and dressing, shopping, collecting pension.
2. Laundry Service: see also previous mention under Health Services. This is run by the Social Services Department in some areas.
3. The Social Services Department will advise about alterations and adaptations to the home which may make it easier for a disabled person to manage — for instance if the bathroom or lavatory is inaccessible. If the house belongs to the Council this will be done in consultation with the Housing Department. The Social Services Department will advise and help about alterations to privately owned or rented houses.

4. It may be possible for a holiday to be arranged for the incontinent person. The Central Council for the Disabled issues an annual guide 'Holidays for the Physically Handicapped' in which details are given of holiday accommodation where incontinent guests are accepted. Some organisations also run their own holiday homes. The social worker will advise and help with arrangements.

5. Equipment such as commodes, chemical closets and special chairs can also be supplied. The Red Cross and St. John Ambulance Brigade may lend equipment at short notice for a temporary period.

The address of the Social Services Department can be obtained from the local Town Hall or Post Office, or from the doctor or nurse, or found in the telephone directory.

FINANCIAL HELP

Constant Attendance Allowance: this is a tax-free allowance for those who require a considerable amount of care during the day or night, or both. Supplementary Benefits — Provision for Exceptional Needs: for anyone already receiving a supplementary allowance or pension there may be an additional allowance payable for extra expenses incurred such as those on heating and laundry. Payment may also be made for replacement of items such as bedding, floor covering or clothing. Enquiries about financial aid should be made at the local Social Security Office, the address of which will be found in the Post Office. For those unable to call at their local office, a visit at home can be requested.

12

Conclusions

In this small book I have attempted to look at and discuss the subject of incontinence in the hope that the reader will be able to understand the problem and know what kind of help to seek. No one solution exists.

Medical matters are commonly written about in the press and discussed on television and radio. If incontinence were included sufferers would feel less isolated. A wider knowledge among professionals about the physical and emotional aspects of incontinence, whether in hospital, in other institutions or in the home would lead to more positive management and even prevention. Physiotherapeutic measures could be further explored with advantage.

Some sufferers require specialist urological investigation but at present this is not available in all areas. In a few centres a number of allied specialists are working together on the problem (guidance and information about these can be obtained from the Disabled Living Foundation). A few years ago a medical society was formed called the International Continence Society* in which urologists, gynaecologists, geriatricians and physiologists meet periodically in an attempt to solve the problems of incontinence.

A variety of protective equipment exists and information regarding this should be more readily available. Requirements for the varying forms of incontinence as well as for different types of patients need to be 'spelt out' for manufacturers and to the Supplies Officers of the Area Health Authorities.

Nearly one hundred million underpads are said to be supplied annually by the Health Service. This is not an effective answer to the incontinence problem and it is certainly not an economic one.

---

*Address given in Appendix D.

Appendix C

BOOKS FOR FURTHER READING

Adult Bedwetters and their Problems.	Harry Stone. The Cyrenians Ltd. 13 Wincheap, Canterbury, Kent, 1973.
Cleanliness and Godliness.	Reginald Reynolds. Allen and Unwin, 1943.
Clothes Sense for Handicapped Adults of all Ages.	P. Macartney. Disabled Living Foundation, 1973.
Clothing for the Handicapped Child.	Gillian Forbes. Disabled Living Foundation.
Coping With Disablement.	Peggy Jay. Consumers' Association, 1974.
Dressing for Disabled People	Rosemay Ruston SRN SCM HV Disabled Living Foundation 1977.
Geriatric Nursing.	E. M. Burns, B. Isaacs and T. Gracie. William Heinemann Medical Books Ltd., 1973. (useful for both relatives and nurses)

Management of Incontinence in the Home — A Survey.	Patricia Dobson. Disabled Living Foundation, 1974.
My Brother's Keeper?	Monnica C. Stewart. Health Horizon Ltd. Chest and Heart Association, Tavistock House North, London WC1, 1968.
Portable Urinals and Related Appliances — A guide to Availability and Use.	Peter Lowthian. Disabled Living Foundation, 1975.
Regaining Bladder Control.	E. Montgomery. John Wright and Sons, 1974.
Urinary Incontinence.	Edited by K. P. S. Caldwell. Sector Publishing Ltd. 70 Chiswick High Road, London W4, 1975. (A medical textbook)

Appendix D

ADDRESSES OF SOME USEFUL ORGANISATIONS

Association for Spina Bifida and Hydrocephalus, 30 Devonshire Street, London W1 2EB.

British Epilepsy Association, 3–6 Alfred Place, London WC1E 7ED.

British Red Cross Society, 9 Grosvenor Crescent, London SW1X 7EJ.

Central Council for the Disabled, 34 Eccleston Square, London SW1V 1PE.

Chest, Heart and Stroke Association, Tavistock House North, Tavistock Square, London WC1H 9JE.

Colostomy Welfare Group, 38–39 Eccleston Square, London SW1V 1PD.

Disabled Living Foundation, 346 Kensington High Street, London W14 8NS.

Disablement Income Group (DIG), Atlee House, Toynbee Hall, Commercial Street, London E1 6LR.

Ileostomy Association of Great Britain and N. Ireland, Drove Cottage, Fuzzy Drove, Kempshott, Basingstoke, Hants.

International Continence Society, Hon. Sec. E. S. Glen FRCS, Dept. of Urology, Southern General Hospital, Glasgow.

Invalid Children's Aid Association, 126 Buckingham Palace Road, London SW1W 95B.

Multiple Sclerosis Society, 4 Tachbrook Street, London SW1X 8TR.

Muscular Dystrophy Group of Great Britain, Nattrass House, 35 Macaulay Road, London SW4 0QP.

National Society for Mentally Handicapped Children, Pembridge Hall, 17 Pembridge Square, London W2 4EP.

Spastics Society, 12 Park Crescent, London W1N 4EQ.

Spinal Injuries Association, King's Fund Centre, 126 Albert Street, Camden, London NW1 7NE.

St. John Ambulance, 1 Grosvenor Crescent, London SW1.
Thistle Foundation, 22 Charlotte Square, Edinburgh EH2 4DF.
(for enquiries in Scotland)

Aids Centres:

Newcastle-upon-Tyne Council for the Disabled, Mea House, Ellison Place, Newcastle-upon-Tyne NE1 8XS.
Disabled Living Centre, 84 Suffolk Street, Birmingham B1.
Merseyside Aids Centre, Youens Way, East Brescott Road, Liverpool 14.
Scottish Information Service for the Disabled (SISD), Claremont House, 18–19 Claremont Crescent, Edinburgh EH7 4RD.

Glossary

ALIMENTARY CANAL: the whole channel through which food passes from the mouth to the anus.

ANUS: back passage. A ring-like opening at the end of the bowel through which solid faeces are finally passed.

ARTERY: a muscular tube conveying blood from the heart to all parts of the body.

BLADDER: a bag-like structure in which urine is collected. It lies in the pelvis in front of the bowel.

BOWEL: also called intestine. The alimentary canal below the stomach through which food travels to the anus. It is 33 ft. long in the average adult.

CATHETER: a thin flexible tube introduced into the bladder to withdraw urine.

COMA: deep unconsciousness.

CONGENITAL: dating from birth.

CONTINENCE: the ability to control bladder and bowel functions.

CYSTITIS: infection of the bladder.

DETRUSOR: emptying muscle of the bladder.

DIURETIC: a substance such as a drug which stimulates the kidneys to produce urine (water pills).

DOUBLE INCONTINENCE: a condition where both urinary and faecal incontinence exist.

DRIBBLING: a flow of urine in drops or a trickling stream.

ENURESIS: usually applied to bedwetting children, but can also apply to adults.

EXCRETA: waste expelled from the body i.e. urine and faeces.

FAECES: waste matter emptied from the bowel; sometimes called a motion or stool.

FIBROIDS: benign growths in the womb.

GYNAECOLOGY: the study of disease of women, especially of the reproductive system.

GERIATRICS: the study of the health and welfare of old people.

INFECTION: disease-producing germs on or in the body.

INTESTINE (see BOWEL): bowel from stomach to anus.

LAX: loose, relaxed.

MICTURITION: urination, passing water.

OVERFLOW INCONTINENCE: dribbling urine from an over-full bladder.

PELVIS: bony basin at lower end of the spine.

PELVIC FLOOR: two flat sheets of muscle which approximate in the mid line, and through which the urethra, the vagina (female) and the bowel pass.

PENIS: the male organ through which the urethra passes.

POLYURIA: production of large quantities of urine.

PRECIPITANCY: passing of urine with awareness but no warning.

PROLAPSE: slipping forward or down of part of an organ such as the womb or rectum.

PROSTATE: a gland in men which lies below the bladder and surrounds the upper part of the urethra.

RECTUM: the final part of the bowel which terminates in the anus.

REFLEX: an automatic response.

SCROTUM: bag containing the testicles.

SIGN: evidence of disease which the doctor observes.

SYMPTOM: that which the patient is aware of.

SPINAL CORD: a rope-like mass of nerve cells and fibres which can transmit messages from the brain and the tissues of the body.

SPHINCTER: ring of muscle guarding or closing an opening in the body i.e. anal sphincter.

STOMA: small mouth-like opening made artificially from a hollow organ like the bowel or bladder to the skin surface.

STRESS INCONTINENCE: a small leakage of urine which occurs on any unusual exertion such as coughing, laughing or sneezing.

STROKE: paralysis arising from brain damage.

TRAUMA: injury.

TRIGONE: triangular shaped base of the bladder.

URETERS: two tubes which convey urine from the kidneys to the bladder.

URETHRA: the outlet pipe from the bladder. 1½″ in the female, and 6″ − 8″ in the male.

URGENCY: a pressing and urgent desire to pass water.

URINE: fluid from the kidneys stored in the bladder and voided through the urethra at intervals.

URINATE: to pass urine.

URINARY DIVERSION: a method of emptying urine through an artificial opening made in the wall of the abdomen, or by transplanting the ureters into the wall of the bowel.

URINARY RETENTION: inability to pass urine, and consequent over-filling of the bladder.

UROLOGY: study of diseases of the urinary system.

UTERUS: womb. The female organ within which the child is conceived, situated between the bladder and the rectum.

UTERINE: connected with the uterus.

VAGINA: front passage in the female leading to the uterus.

WOMB: see uterus.

Index